TO BE A PIONEER

TO BE A PIONEER

PAUL C. BURNS AND RUTH HINES

ILLUSTRATED BY FRANK ALOISE

ABINGDON PRESS: NEW YORK AND NASHVILLE

FOR TODAY'S CHILDREN—TOMORROW'S PIONEERS

CONTENTS

TO BE A PIONEER

THE PIONEER

Down through the centuries as people have gathered together to live in settled communities, there have always been some who have become dissatisfied with life in the community and set out to find a better life elsewhere. After the discovery of America, many of the more adventurous ones left their homes in Europe to find freedom and a new way of living in the new land. They built their homes and developed farms in the areas along the coastline. Before many years had passed, the land became more thickly settled and towns, cities, and factories grew up. Again there were men who left to find better land farther to the west. They crossed the mountains to build new homes in the wilderness. As the years passed, this land, too, became so thickly settled

9

that it was no longer a wilderness; and the westward movement continued, across the Mississippi River to the great plains, and on across the Rockies to the Pacific coast. Those who went first were known as pioneers. They were strong and courageous people. With none of the conveniences that seem so necessary today, they learned to make the best use of what they had.

It is hard for people today to imagine what life was like for the pioneer. In the settled areas from which he came, there were shops and factories as well as farms. Many conveniences were available which made life comfortable; but the pioneer could take with him when he left only the things which were necessary—an axe, a rifle, a few farm tools, seeds, cooking utensils, blankets, a small supply of food and clothing.

When he had selected a place to settle, he made his own shelter from whatever materials he found at hand —the trees of the forest, or the sod of the prairie. The nearest neighbor might be miles away; the nearest store, which had a very limited stock, was much more distant. All the food for the family had to be grown on the land or hunted in the forests. Clothing was made at home. Every one in the family—father, mother, and all but the youngest children—had to work hard to provide the things they needed. There were only the simplest of tools to help with this work.

The pioneer people became skilled in doing many things. They found ways to preserve food in summer for use in winter. They learned to use materials that might otherwise have been wasted to add to the comfort of their homes. Some of the pioneer arts have almost vanished. Others are practiced to this day, though a bit differently.

THE WESTWARD MOVEMENT

Pioneers first went west from Pennsylvania, New York, and other states in the East or on the Atlantic coast. They went to the land beyond the Appalachian Mountains. The journey was long and hard, sometimes taking four or five months. The first travelers used footpaths and trails made by animals and by the Indians. The trails often followed streams so that it would be easy to get water. Gradually these trails were widened into roads of a sort. These roads were very rough and crude compared to the roads of today. The names of the most famous trails come easily to mind: Wilderness, Cumberland, and others. Later pioneers left the East and the Middle West to go to the Far West. They traveled on the Sante Fe Trail, The Oregon Trail and other paths, blazed by trappers and hunters.

Pioneers traveled over land on foot, on horseback, by pack horse, and by covered wagon. They brought with them food, livestock, seeds, and a few pieces of household equipment. They could not carry nearly all the things they needed. The Conestoga wagon was popular because it could carry a whole family and many of their belongings. This wagon was curved upward

at each end so things did not fall out when it tipped or
tilted on the rough roads. Sometimes as many as twenty
or thirty wagons joined together to form a caravan or
wagon train. They faced many dangers and difficulties
—bad roads, Indian attacks, wagon breakdowns, sickness, bad weather, loss of oxen and other livestock.

Many pioneers traveled to their new homes over the
rivers by raft, flatboat, keelboat, and later by steam-
boat. Some men tied logs together to make rafts to

carry their families, livestock, and household goods. Flatboats had a sort of boxlike house in the center which gave shelter on the journey. Travel by water was easier than travel by land in some ways, but there were also many dangers and hardships such as sandbars, whirlpools and rapids, snags, floating logs, and high or low water. And just as on land, there were Indian attacks, sickness, and bad weather.

The pioneer felt that the new life in the new land would be worth all the hardships. In the East he had felt crowded. In the West, he had heard, game and fish were plentiful. He could hunt and trap and explore as he pleased. The rich soil would grow fine crops and provide a good living for his family.

CHOOSING A SITE FOR A HOME

The land on which the pioneers settled belonged to the government and was sold very cheaply. Until about the year 1862, the usual price was two dollars or less per acre. The settler could get land by paying about a fourth of the total cost at first and the rest in yearly payments. In some areas the pioneer could get the land free by agreeing to stay on it a certain number of years. He looked for a place where there was good soil and plenty of water and timber. When he found land which pleased him, he staked a claim. He measured the land for his claim by paces. A pace is the length of a good-sized step by an adult or about one yard. Eighty-four paces each way made an acre. Fifteen hundred paces each way made 320 acres. A claim was often 160 or 320 acres. The corners of the claim were marked in different ways—with a big rock, a stake with a sign, or a mound of dirt. A stream or a row of trees might be used to mark the boundary of a claim. There were not many quarrels over land since there was plenty for everyone.

Measure an Acre

You might like to measure an acre yourself, in your school yard or in a park, by pacing as the pioneers did. Use a stone or some other object to mark your starting place. Two "giant steps" would be about the same length as one pace. Beginning at your starting point, walk 84 paces (168 "giant steps") in a straight line. Mark the end of the line with a stone. Turn and take 84 more paces at right angles to the first line. Again mark the corner. Make a right angle turn and take another 84 paces. Mark the end of this line and then return to your first marker. The square you have paced will be about one acre.

BUILDING A HOUSE

After the settler had chosen his land and staked his claim, he had to build a house for his family and himself. He was not always able to do this right away. Some families camped in tents until a house could be built. Others lived in caves or big trees. Some used the covered wagon as a sleeping place, and meals were prepared out of doors. Some lived in dugouts. A dugout was a hole dug in a hillside and then covered over with a roof of poles and brush.

As soon as possible, the pioneer man began to cut down trees and clear a space for his cabin. The cabin usually consisted of one room. Four big logs were placed down for the foundation. The men notched the ends of the logs and fitted them together. The logs used for many of the cabins were about 20 feet long for the sides and 16 feet long for the ends. Cracks between the logs were filled with mud, moss, and sticks. This was called chinking or daubing. Some logs were

split in half with a frow, a tool something like an ax. These split logs with the face smoothed were called puncheons. Puncheons were used to make the floor of the cabin. Clapboards (boards something like small puncheons) were used for the roof of the cabin. The chimney was made of stone and mud, and the windows of greased paper or greased deerskin. The finished cabin stood about 7 or 8 feet tall. It was very hard for one man to build a cabin alone, so neighbors usually helped each other. A gathering of neighbors for the purpose of building a house was called a house raising.

On the prairies where trees were scarce many sod houses were built. Sod is topsoil held together by the matted roots of grass and weeds. Strips or blocks of sod were put together like building blocks to make the walls of the house. The roof was made of poles and brush covered with more layers of sod. The floor was just hard-packed dirt. A man could build a sod house in about a week with only a spade.

Make a Pioneer Latch

A pioneer house did not have a lock on the door, but it did have a latch and a latchstring. The latchstring passed through a hole in the door. It was a string of deerhide and was attached to a bar on the inside of the door. The bar was fastened to the door and rested in a piece of wood on the door joint, locking the door. Pulling the latchstring raised the bar so the door could be opened. At night the latchstring was pulled inside. You can use cardboard for your door, doorframe, and bar when you make your latch.

19

FURNISHING THE CABIN

Most of the furniture in the pioneer cabin was made at home. It was rough and crude. It was made from hard woods that grew in nearby forests such as black walnut, oak, or hickory. Even dishes for family use were made of wood.

A large stump sometimes served as a table, but usually a table top was made by fastening puncheons together with wooden pegs. The table top was placed on legs stuck in auger holes on the round side of the puncheon. A bench was made by using a longer puncheon. A cradle might be made of a hollow log put on rockers. A rug of bearskin was often found in front of the fireplace.

A shelf was made by putting wooden pegs in the wall and laying a clapboard over them. A cupboard was simply a group of shelves.

To make a bed, some pioneers put a forked stick in the floor at the proper distance from the wall. They laid poles from the stick to the wall. Then they covered the poles with woven branches or skins. Quilts and skins were piled on this. Later, if geese were raised by the family, geese feathers were used to fill feather beds and feather pillows. Baby's trundle bed was usually out of sight beneath the big bed.

Part of the furnishings of every cabin was a flintlock rifle usually placed on deer antlers hung on the wall. The bullet pouch, powder-horn (just a hollowed-out cow horn), and mold for making bullets were always nearby.

Making a Stool or Bench

You can make a miniature pioneer bench from a small tree branch. Find a dead branch on a low tree or a large bush. With a knife or a small saw cut off the branch. Then cut off a short piece of the branch at the thickest end. Saw or cut the small piece in half. This is a puncheon. With your knife, or with a drill or auger, if your father has one and will let you use it, make four holes, two at each end of the puncheon on the curved side. Place twigs or small sticks, all the same length, into the holes. Now you have a miniature stool or bench.

THE FIREPLACE—
THE CENTER OF THE PIONEER HOME

A most important place in the pioneer home was the fireplace. A fire was kept burning all the time. In winter the log fire gave both heat and light. The cooking was done at the fireplace.

Every fireplace in a pioneer home contained the following things:

1. Andirons—iron rods standing before the fire to keep the coals from falling out on the hearth
2. Backlogs—large pieces of green wood placed in back of the fireplace to protect the walls
3. Bellows—an instrument used to fan the fire
4. Crane—a swinging rod on which kettles were hung over the fire
5. Dutch oven—a heavy covered iron kettle
6. Hearth—the part of the floor directly in front of the fire
7. Mantle—the shelf at the top of the fireplace
8. Spit—a rod on which meats were roasted
9. Tongs—tools used to pick up hot coals

PROVIDING WATER FOR THE HOME

A good supply of water was very important to the pioneer. Sometimes a spring or a river near his land provided plenty of water, but sometimes he had to carry the water from long distances by means of a yoke over his shoulders.

Often a well had to be dug. Digging a well was not easy because there were not many tools available for digging—only shovels, spades, and picks.

A water witch was sometimes used to decide where to dig a well. The water witch was a forked stick that was supposed to bend down when held over a place where there was water underground. Many people really believed that the stick could tell them where to find water.

When the well was dug, there were several ways of getting the water out. One was a well sweep. The sweep was a long pole laid over a stick. The large end of the pole was held down by a heavy object such as a

24

stone. A bucket was fastened to the smaller end. It could be easily raised or lowered.

A pulley was also used sometimes to get the water out. The pulley was fastened over the well. A rope was put around the groove in the pulley. On one end of the rope was the bucket. The rope went through the pulley and let the bucket down into the well. Pulling on the other end of the rope brought the bucket back.

The windlass was another way of getting water. The windlass was a large spool turned by a crank. A rope around the spool had a bucket fastened on the end. The bucket could be raised or lowered by turning the crank.

Pioneers often kept a rainbarrel outside the house to catch rain water which was used for bathing and washing.

Make a Pioneer Well and Dipper

To make a well, you will need a quart paper milk carton, an empty thread spool, two slender twigs, and some twine. Cut off the top of the milk carton. Then cut a hole in each of two sides of the carton, across from each other. Slide the twig through the hole on one side, then run the twig through the hole in the spool and through the hole on the other side of the carton. Wrap some twine around one end of the twig very tightly so that twig cannot slip out of place. Tie the second twig tightly at right angles to the other end of the first twig. Now tie a long piece of twine to the spool, and if you have something to use for a bucket tie it to the other end. When you turn the "handle" at the end of the twig, the bucket will go up and down.

Gourds of the thin-walled or dipper type (used by pioneers for drinking from the water bucket) can be easily cut or carved when mature but not thoroughly dried. Cut a hole of the desired shape and size in the gourd. Throw away the seeds and other material found in the center of the gourd. If well cleaned and dried, gourds of this type are firm, light, and durable.

26

LIGHTING THE HOME

At first some families had only the light from their fireplaces. A few people burned pine knots or candlewood. Pine knots were the part of the pine tree where the branch grew out of the trunk. They were full of oil or pitch and burned brightly. They were usually burned in the fireplace or over a flat stone so that the sticky pitch would not drip on the floor. The inside of the trunk of the pine tree was called candlewood. It was cut into little sticks that were burned for light. Pine knots and candlewood made a smoky, dripping light because of the pitch in them, but they gave more light than other kind of burning wood.

The inside or pith of plants called rushes was sometimes soaked in grease and burned. Such a light was called a rushlight.

As soon as they could, the people tried to make lamps. An early lamp was made by placing a wick (string twisted around a stick) in an open dish or saucer filled with some sort of grease or oil. This was called a "saucer lamp." If there was no dish that could be used for a lamp, a vegetable lamp was made by hollowing out a turnip, beet, or potato and putting in a wick. Then the hole was filled with grease and the wick was set afire. Some lamps were made of metal or clay. Some had spouts in which to put the wick, and chains or hooks so that they could be hung. The hooks could be stuck in the log wall of the cabin. Some of these lamps were called Betty lamps.

Candles were made of tallow or beeswax molded into shape with a wick down the center. Tallow is the hard fat from sheep, cows, or deer. Sometimes beeswax was added to tallow to make the candle harder. In the East, bayberry candles were made from the oily berries of the bayberry bush; but in the West tallow candles were most common. The wick or string in the middle of the candle was made of spun flax or hemp. Later cotton wicks were used. If nothing else was available, even the silk from milkweed was twisted into candle wicks.

Most of the candles were used in the winter. In the summer people got up very early and then went to bed when it was too dark to see without a light. Even in winter, candles might not be used except for very special occasions.

Candles were sometimes placed in lanterns which could be carried from place to place. Some lanterns had glass sides. Other lanterns were made of tin with little holes through which the light came.

Candles were actually made in several ways. One method was to dip a piece of string called the wick into hot tallow or wax. It was dipped again and again. Each time it was dipped, a little more wax or tallow stuck to the wick until the candle was the desired size.

These candles were not made one at a time. Wicks were doubled, twisted, and hung on smooth wooden sticks called candle rods. Six or eight wicks were put on each rod. Two straight back chairs were set with the backs facing each other. Two long poles were placed parallel to each other across the backs of the chairs. The candle rods were laid across the poles like the rungs on a ladder. Boards were laid on the floor underneath to catch any wax that dripped down.

Tallow was melted in a big kettle. Enough hot water was added to make the tallow come up almost to the top of the kettle.

Two people sat down with the kettle between them. They took turns dipping the wicks on the candle rods into the tallow. The wicks were let down until the rod was even with the top of the kettle. Then the rod was lifted slowly up. After each rod of wicks was dipped it was hung on the poles to cool and harden.

After the wicks were dipped the first time, they were sometimes crooked. They had to be straightened by hand. This was called stripping. The wicks were dipped over and over. Each time the candles became a little larger. After twenty or thirty dippings they were the correct size. Candles that were too large smoked when they were burned.

The candles were left on the rods and poles until they were cold and hard. Then they were carefully taken off. They were packed in candle boxes and put

where mice could not get to them. Mice liked to eat tallow candles.

A good candlemaker could make about two hundred candles in one day. Candlemaking was done in cool weather so the candles would get hard faster.

Molded candles were not as hard to make as dipped candles. The candle mold was made of two to twelve hollow tin tubes fastened together. There was a little hole in the bottom of each tube. The top end was open.

The wick was cut so that it was a little more than two times as long as the mold. It was doubled and put into the mold. A wire or stick was put through the looped ends at the top of the mold. This kept the wick in the middle of the tube. The two cut ends of the wicks came through the hole at the bottom. A knot was tied at the ends. The knot had to be big enough to keep the wick from slipping back through the hole. It also kept tallow from running out of the bottom of the mold. Some people stuck a piece of raw potato over the end of each tube instead of tying a knot. The potato held the wick in place and closed the hole.

Tallow or beeswax was melted. A little was poured in the bottom of each tube in the mold. When this tallow hardened, it kept the mold from leaking. After the first tallow hardened, each tube was filled with more melted tallow. The mold was then put in a cool place until the candles were cold and hard.

To take the candles from the mold, the knots at the bottom were cut or the pieces of potato removed. The mold was dipped very quickly into a kettle of hot water. This caused a little of the tallow along the sides of the mold to melt. Then the candles could be lifted out by the stick or wire that went through the loops at the top of the mold.

Make Your Own Light

A Button Lamp

To make a button lamp, you will need a saucer or dish, a piece of cloth about five inches long and five inches wide, a button one inch in diameter, thread, and one tablespoon of fat (lard or tallow). Put the button in the middle of the cloth. Twist the cloth into a long rope, with the button inside the cloth at the bottom. Wind the thread around the twisted cloth to hold it tight. Wind the thread as close down to the button as possible. Then tie the ends of the thread and cut them off. Rub some of the fat over the cloth. Melt the rest of the fat and put it into the saucer. Place the button in the fat. Light the top of the cloth as you would a candle. Add more fat when the first is almost gone.

Dipping Candles

It is fun to dip candles. Here is an easy way to do it in almost the same way that the pioneers did it. To make one dipped candle you will need a length of wicking or soft string about six inches longer than you want your candle to be when finished, a short straight stick (about 12 inches is a good length), and two tall, wide-mouthed jars or cans (tall juice cans are good). Cover the space where you are working with newspapers. In a saucepan melt enough paraffin, with a little beeswax added if you can get it, to fill one of the cans. If you like, you can color the wax by adding crayons of the desired color. Have your mother or father or some older person pour the wax into one of the cans and set the can in a pan of boiling water. Be very careful in handling the hot wax. Fill the second can with cold water and put the can in a pan of ice cubes. Tie one end of the string or wick around the center of the stick. Dip the wick in the hot wax. Take it out and let it harden in the air. Then dip it in the cold water and drain completely. Dip it again in the hot wax and then in the cold water. Dip over and over until the candle is as large as you wish. If the wax in the can begins to harden before the dipping is completed, reheat it and also reheat the water in the pan. When the candle is completely hard, cut the string and remove it from the stick.

MAKING CLOTHING

Pioneers made their own clothing at home; there was little "store" clothing. Skins and furs were used a great deal. A loose deerskin shirt, somewhat like those of the Indians, was worn by many of the men. Deerskin moccasins were common footwear. Caps were often made of raccoon or fox skins with the tails left hanging down in back for decoration.

Pioneer women knew how to make cloth. Where sheep were raised cloth was made of wool. After the wool was sheared from the sheep, the women washed, combed and carded it into smooth silky strands. Then they used a spinning wheel to twist the strands of wool into thread.

Flax was also used to make cloth. Flax came from a plant that grew in swamps. The stems of the plant were soaked and separated into strands which were then made into thread on a spinning wheel. A large wheel was used for spinning wool and a smaller wheel for flax. Cloth that is made from flax is called linen.

Thread was woven into cloth on a loom. The cloth was called homespun. Besides pure woolen and pure linen cloth, the pioneers also made linsey-woolsey.

The lengthwise threads of this cloth were linen and the crosswise threads were wool. The linen made it strong and the wool added warmth.

Cloth was dyed with dyes made from plants that were

found in the woods and fields. Pioneers made dyes from blueberries (berry), beets (roots), goldenrod (flower), black walnuts (husks), alder (bark), wild cherry (bark), sumac (berries), birch (dry leaves), bloodroot (roots), lily of the valley (stalks and leaves), elderberry (fruit), and other plants.

Cloth dyed with these dyes faded when washed or left in the sun, but the pioneers found that certain things would set the dye and keep it from fading. These were called *mordants*. Salt, vinegar, alum, and lye were commonly used as mordants. Mordants also changed some colors. Salt made some colors lighter, alum made some darker. Pokeweed berries make a purple color, but with an alum or vinegar mordant they make a red dye. Hemlock bark makes a reddish brown color, but with an alum mordant it makes yellow. The pioneer women tried many different ways of dyeing and learned what to use to make the colors they wanted.

Pioneers also used indigo to dye cloth a pretty blue. Indigo was bought at a store or from a man called the indigo peddler who went from cabin to cabin selling it. It is made from plants that grow in India, Java, Natal, and the southern part of the United States. It has been used as a dye for thousands of years.

Dyes You Can Make

Beet dye

Red dye can be made from beets. Wash about 4 ounces of beets. Cut them into little pieces. Soak overnight in enough water to cover them. Boil for 1 hour. Strain. Pour the liquid and 6 cups of water into an enamel pan. Use wool material that has been soaked in a vinegar mordant. (1 cup vinegar; 4 cups of warm water.) If the material is dry, wet it. Put it into the dye and simmer for 1 hour. Stir it all the time with a stick. Be sure not to twist the material or stir it into a ball. Take the material out of the dye and rinse it in warm water. Then rinse in cooler waters until the water stays clear. Wash in soapy water after rinsing. Rinse again. Squeeze the water out of the material. Do not wring or twist it. Roll the material in an old towel or cloth to soak up the water. Hang it up to dry in the shade.

Iris dye

Here is a recipe for making purple dye as the pioneer did it. You will need to do this in the spring when the irises are blooming. Be sure to get permission to pick the irises, if you try it.

Pick about four ounces of purple iris petals. Soak them overnight in enough water to cover them. Then boil the petals for one hour. Strain and pour the liquid into an enamel pan. Add six cups of water. The dye is ready for use. Choose material for dyeing that has been soaked in a mordant. (The vinegar mordant mentioned for the red beet dye is fine.) Wet the material. Put it into the dye and simmer for one hour, stirring it all the time with a stick. Be sure not to twist the material or stir it into a ball. Take the material out of the dye and rinse it in warm water. Then rinse in cool water until the water stays clear. Squeeze the water out of the material. Do not wring or twist. Roll the material in an old towel or cloth to soak up some of the water. Unroll and hang the material in the shade to dry.

MAKING PATCHWORK QUILTS

The early pioneer cabins were cold and drafty in winter. The heat from the fireplace did not warm the whole house. Plenty of warm bedcovers were needed to keep the family comfortable on cold winter nights. To meet this need, the pioneer women made bedcoverings known as quilts.

A quilt is made by stitching together two layers of cloth with a layer of a soft, warm substance such as wool or cotton between them. Since cloth was very scarce in pioneer days, the women saved every scrap of material left over from making clothing and the best parts of worn-out or out-grown garments. Pieces were cut from these scraps and were sewn together to make the top layer of the quilt. This kind of quilt was a patchwork quilt. Sewing the pieces together to make the top was called piecing the quilt.

When quilts were needed in a hurry, the women would sew the pieces together in a hit or miss fashion, the result being known as a "crazy quilt." When there was more time and more material to choose from, the pieces were cut into squares, rectangles, diamonds, triangles, and other shapes, and then put together to make beautiful designs. Color schemes were planned with great care. The loveliest of these quilts were considered too fine for everyday use and were brought out only for very special occasions such as the visit of the circuit rider. The everyday quilts were soon worn out from much use, but the more beautiful ones lasted a very long time. Some families today have one or more beautiful quilts made many, many years ago. Many women still make quilts today, not because of a need for this kind of bed covering, but because they enjoy doing it.

Winter was the time for piecing quilts. There was less work to do at this season, and the weather was such that much time had to be spent indoors. The women and girls stayed busy by working on quilts. Cutting the pieces and sewing them together took a long time. The pieces were first sewed together in blocks which formed the basis of the design. The pieced blocks were then set together with alternating plain squares or strips between, or joined together to make an all-over design.

Quilt patterns were exchanged by pioneer women. Many made their own designs or changed other designs to suit themselves. The simplest patterns were based on the square. The easiest was the four-patch made of four pieces alternating light and dark. Cutting each of the four-patch squares diagonally made a windmill design. Another favorite was the nine-patch pattern.

A more difficult design was the honeycomb. When done with careful attention to color harmony this produced a mosaic effect.

When the quilt top was finished, there still remained the task of quilting. A piece of plain material a little larger than the quilt top was placed in a frame to hold it tight, called a quilting frame. Then the filler (cotton or wool) was spread carefully and evenly over the material and tacked down. Finally the top was put into place. The three layers were sewed together with tiny even stitches. Sometimes these stitches were done in a fancy pattern.

However they were done, the rows of stitching were quite close together so that the pieces would be firmly held. This was a most important step, and the pioneer woman felt disgraced if the top was puckered or uneven.

Since there was not room to leave the quilt spread out completely, and since it would not be possible to reach all parts of the quilt if it were left in this position, the frames were made so that the quilt could be rolled up, leaving a portion exposed for quilting. As one part was finished, it was rolled up and a new portion was exposed. Quilting required skill in sewing. Some quilting designs were very simple, but other designs were quite elaborate.

Quilting bees were common social events, especially in the spring. The women and girls completed their quilt tops during the winter. In the spring, invitations were sent out to neighbors and friends to come for a day of quilting. The guests arrived early in the morning and began to work at once. They marked the quilting design and started the actual quilting. As they worked, they exchanged news and neighborhood gossip. At about eleven o'clock lunch was served. The hostesses prepared all their special dishes, and many of the women exchanged recipes. After lunch the work went on until five or six o'clock when the men of the various families arrived for supper. The men enjoyed an opportunity for talk. The evening often ended with games and dancing.

Have a Quilting Bee

You might like to piece a quilt block. Choose the design you wish to use. Make patterns of the pieces you need from heavy cardboard. Choose scraps of material in colors that go well together. Most designs work out best with a light and a dark color or a solid color and a print. Lay your pattern on the wrong side of the cloth and trace around it lightly with a soft pencil. Cut the pieces ¼ inch outside the pencil lines. Sew the pieces together with small stitches. The pencil marks will be your guide lines for sewing.

A quilt block can be used to make a nice pot holder. Cut a piece of plain material the size of the block. Place an even layer of cotton on the wrong side of this piece. Lay the pieced block on the top. Work out your own design for quilting the block. Bind the sides of the block with bias binding.

Quilting Patterns

Four Patch Design

To make this design you need two patterns, one of the large square and one of the small. For each block cut two large squares (4″) of plain material, four small squares (2″) of dark material and four small squares of light material.

Windmill Design

This block requires only one pattern. Cut four light and four dark triangles (4″) for each block.

Nine Patch Design

All squares are the same size (3″). Cut five of dark material and four of light.

MAKING BRAIDED RUGS

Another use for discarded or outgrown clothing was the rag rug which added warmth and color to cold bare floors. Every scrap of cloth was saved regardless of the material—wool, linen, linsey-woolsey, and cotton all went into the same rug. The material was cut into strips. Sometimes the strips were woven to make rugs, but more often they were braided. Braiding was preferred because no special equipment was needed. A frame or loom was not necessary. A flat-iron, sometimes called a sad-iron, or some other heavy object was used to hold the ends of the braid on a table and help keep the tension even. When the braid was long enough, some women held the end of the braid to the floor with one foot and wound the braid around a chair

and pulled it across the straight chair back. Other women found that they could make a tight even braid more easily if they sat with feet braced against the lower rung of the chair and tied the end of the braid to the chair.

Some rugs were made of scraps put together without any particular design. When there was much to do, this was the easiest and quickest way to make the rug. When it was possible, however, more attention was given to making the rug a thing of beauty. A color scheme was worked out and materials were carefully sorted and dyed in the chosen colors.

Braid Your Own Rug

To make a braided rug, select pieces of material in colors you would like to use or simply use any scraps you have. Cut your material into strips about 1 ½ inches wide. Begin your braid with three strips that are of different lengths so that when new pieces are added all the seams will not come at the same place. Fasten the ends of the strips together with a safety pin. Braid as girls braid their pigtails. Bring the first strip across the second, the third across the first, then the second across the third. Repeat over and over. Turn the edges of the strips under as you braid so that the raw edges of the material will not show on the outside. When you come almost to the end of your shortest strip fasten the braid with a safety pin. Sew on another strip.

Continue braiding and adding strips until you have as much braid as you need for your rug. It can be as small or as large as you wish. It may be round or oval, whichever you prefer. Lay your braid flat on a table wrong side up. Shape it the way you want it, and sew together on the wrong side.

The husks of corn may also be braided into mats. First the husks must be thoroughly dried. Husks dried indoors out of the sun are a soft green color. Those dried in the sun are bleached almost white. For braiding, discard the coarse outer husks and use the softer inner ones. Tear the husks into narrow strips. Dampen the strips by soaking them in a pan of water for a few minutes. Start the braid by tying together three strips of unequal length. Hook them over a nail or pin them to a board at the knot to help keep the braid firm. For a flat braid keep the strips flat and fold them over carefully. For a round braid, twist the strips as you braid.

When the strips have been braided to within two inches of the end of the shortest strip, a new piece must be added. Let the end of the new piece overlap the first one by two inches. Continue to braid the strips so that the new piece is fastened securely in. As the cornhusk strips are short, new pieces must be added frequently in this same way. It is important to start the braid with strips of unequal length so that new pieces will not need to be added to all three strips at the same time making the braid too bulky. When the braid is completed, any uneven ends that stick out may be trimmed off. To sew the braid together, use a medium-sized needle and a matching or contrasting color of thread. Place the braid on a flat surface and shape as desired. A round shape is probably easiest. Wind the braid to make a spiral center and stitch together. Continue to wind and sew the braid until the mat is the desired size. Be sure to keep it flat.

MAKING SOAP

Making soap in pioner days was a hard job. Soap was made from fats and lye. All kinds of fat were saved for soap-making. The ends of tallow candles, deer and bear

49

oil, and other fats went into the grease barrel. Salt was taken out of the grease by washing it in hot water and letting it stand until the clean grease came to the top, leaving the salt in the water at the bottom.

Lye for the soap was also made at home. Ashes from hardwoods such as oak and hickory were saved in a barrel which had clean straw on the bottom. When water was poured in at the top of the barrel and allowed to trickle through the ashes an alkaline solution called lye was formed. The lye dripped through a small hole at the bottom of the barrel and was collected in a bucket or barrel placed beneath the ash barrel. The lye was tested by putting an egg into it. If the egg floated, the lye was just strong enough to use. This way of making lye was called leaching.

Soap was made in the spring with the grease and ashes saved during the winter. It took about 24 pounds of fat and the lye from six barrels of wood ashes to make a barrel of soft soap. Lye was put in the soap kettle over an open fire out of doors. The grease was slowly added until no more would mix with the lye. Then the soap was cooked until it was jellylike. The mixture had to be stirred for a long time. The children helped with this. Pioneer women were very good at soapmaking and

could tell just how much grease to use and how long
to cook the mixture. When the cooking was finished,
the soap was cooled and stored in barrels. Sometimes
hard soap was also made. To make hard soap a brine or
salt solution was added to the grease and lye. The soap
rose to the top of the kettle. When it had cooled, it
could be cut into bars. A year's supply of soap was
usually made at one time.

THE PIONEER FARM

On the trip West the pioneer had to get along with only the few kinds of food he could carry along and the game, fish, berries, and other foods he could find along the trails.

The pioneer was eager to plant crops as soon as possible. He was very skillful in the use of the axe. With his axe he cut down trees and cleared land for his fields. When the pioneer farmer was ready to clear a new field, he would sometimes kill the trees first by cutting rings around them. Killing trees in this way was called deadening. Another way of making the work go faster was to cut partly through several trees and then cut a large tree which would bring the others down as it fell. The logs were removed to be used later for new buildings, fences, or firewood. Removing the logs from a large space, covered as it often was with undergrowth, was an impossible task for one man. So the neighbors were invited to come for a log-rolling. The men worked with a will to pile the logs together. When the work was finished, they joined the women and children for a hearty supper and an evening of fun.

Once the pioneer had made a clearing, he could plant corn between the stumps if he did not have time to remove them. He used his spade and hoe to prepare the soil. He also made a garden where he planted beans, pumpkins, squash, and other vegetables. He had brought seeds with him from the East or obtained them from a neighbor.

To grow some crops, the land had to be plowed. This meant that the stumps had to be taken out. The axe and mattock were used to loosen the stumps which were pulled out with the help of horses. Removing stumps broke up the soil so that it could be easily plowed.

It was possible to make a plow from a sapling. A fork of the tree could be shaped into a plowshare. Another fork served to fasten the handles together. The iron plowshares which some pioneers brought with them did a better job of plowing, however. Even the iron plow did not work very well on the thick prairie sod. Not until light steel plows were made by John Deere in 1837 was it easy to plow large fields in the plains area.

The pioneer worked hard to produce a good crop, but he faced many difficulties. Not enough rain or too much rain, storms, insects, birds, and animals could ruin his fields. He built fences—stake and rider, worm, stump—to keep out animals. Various types of scarecrows were used to frighten away birds. Some pioneers in the 1830's used a dead hawk tied to a post as a scarecrow.

The pioneer farmer worked from daylight until dark. His tools were not nearly as good as those used on farms today. Only through very hard work was he able to produce almost everything his family needed on his farm. Failure of any crop was very serious as it is for farmers today who face the same problems of drought, insect pests, and plant diseases.

PROVIDING FOOD FOR THE FAMILY

Pioneer families could not go to a store to buy food. They had to grow or hunt for most of the things they ate.

The pioneer needed to be a good hunter. Hunting furnished meat for the family as well as skins that could be tanned and used for making shoes and other articles of clothing. Deer, bears, rabbits, wild turkeys, ducks and geese, prairie chickens, and other wild animals were hunted and killed for meat and hide. Pigs, sheep, cows, and chickens were raised on the farm. The cows and chickens were not killed for they furnished the pioneer with milk and eggs.

Vegetables such as cabbage, turnips, potatoes, pumpkins, onions, and beans, were raised in the garden. Certain wild plants were eaten as greens.

Wild strawberries, blackberries, grapes, plums, and other fruits were picked. The pioneer gathered nuts in the fall.

Honey, maple sugar, and molasses were used to sweeten food.

One method of locating a bee-tree was to smear the smooth surface of a stump with honey. The bees, attracted by the odor, would come to feast on the sweetness. Laden with honey they would make a beeline for their storehouse. The hunters followed the course of the bees until the bee tree was located. The bees were smoked from their shelter with sulphur, the tree chopped down, and the honey brought home. Bee-trees often were located and marked in summer. Later, when the swarm was dormant, the tree was cut down and

carted away. The hunter marked the tree with his initials to insure its protection as his own property against any other claims.

Maple sap was obtained by drilling a hole in each maple tree. A hollow tube made from a branch of an oak tree was put in the hole and a bucket hung upon or below it to catch the sap. When the buckets were nearly filled, they were taken to the cabin to be cooked in a big iron kettle. Here the sap was boiled down to maple syrup. Maple sugar candy and cakes of maple sugar could be made from the syrup.

Sorghum, or "long sweetening," was made at sorghum mills from the stalks of the sorghum plants. The children enjoyed eating the skimmings with a stalk.

Today we have many ways of keeping food from spoiling: freezing, quick canning, dehydrating and others. The pioneers could not do these things in the way we do them, but they did find ways of keeping foods for future use. Some fruits were cooked with a lot of sweetening so they wouldn't spoil as fast. These thick, sweet preserves were put into earthenware jars with covers. Wax was poured around the top to seal out the air. Vinegar and spices were added to foods such as cucumbers and beets. This was called pickling. In some places fruits and vegetables were placed in pits dug in the ground. They were covered with straw and dirt to keep them from freezing and could be taken out when needed. Meat was salted or smoked with hickory wood to preserve it. Venison was jerked by drying out thin strips before the fire. This prevented decay. During the winter meat could be put outside where it was cold enough to keep it from spoiling.

Until good roads were built, pioneers were able to get very few supplies from stores. The nearest store might be quite a distance away and such a long journey could not be made often. Salt was usually bought at the store, and sometimes spices and a little white or "store" sugar, which was used only on special occasions.

The foods most familiar to the pioneer family were: baked beans with salt pork and molasses, vinegar pies, dried apple pies, wild turkey, rabbit stew, dandelion greens, sassafras tea, prairie chicken, hominy, beech nuts, pawpaws, persimmons.

If you visited a pioneer home for the day this might be the menu:

Breakfast

Pancakes, sausage, gravy, milk, applesauce.

Dinner

Hominy, baked beans, johnny cake, head cheese, dried pumpkin or apple pie, milk.

Supper

Rabbit stew, succotash, ash cake or turkey bread, hasty pudding with maple syrup, sassafras tea or milk.

Corn

Nearly every pioneer carried a supply of corn with him when he went West. As soon as possible, he cleared and planted his cornfield, for corn was one of his most important crops. The fresh young ears were used as a vegetable. The ripe kernels were ground into meal and used to prepare many tasty dishes for the family. The ripe grain also provided food for the chickens, the cow, the pigs, and other farm animals. The dried corn cobs could be used for fuel. The husks were dried and braided into mats for floor coverings. The wife often made her broom out of corn husks tied together with a strip of hide. The dried leaves of the plant were stuffed into a bag to serve as a mattress.

A corn husking party was often held when the dried leaves of the corn needed to be stripped off. The pioneers usually assembled in a large barn which was prepared for the occasion; and after each gentleman had selected a lady partner, the husking began. When a lady found a red ear, she was entitled to a kiss from each gentleman present; if a gentleman found one, he was allowed to kiss every lady present. After the corn was all husked, the floor was cleared, the old violin brought out, and the merry dances began, usually lasting until broad daylight.

Until mills were built, corn had to be ground into meal by hand. A mortar and pestle were often used to grind it. A hole was made in a stump or block of wood about a yard high. This was the mortar. The pestle was a block of wood with a handle. It was cut to fit the hole in the mortar. Grain was put into the mortar. The pestle was pounded up and down to grind the grain. Some pestles had two handles so two men, one on each side, could work together.

Some of the settlers worked out another way of grinding corn. When the land was cleared for a cabin, a young sapling was left standing near the cabin door and near the stump of a large tree or a large stone slightly hollowed out on top. A heavy block of wood was fastened to the sapling over the hollow in the stump or rock. A long leather cord was fastened to the top or near the top of the sapling. When the cord was pulled, the heavy block of wood came down on corn placed in the hollow of the stump or stone. The block was pulled down on the corn over and over until the corn was crushed fine enough to use in cooking. The thump of the corn grinding could be heard a long way off. Some of the pioneers "talked" with their far away neighbors as they ground their corn.

Handmills were made of two big, round, flat stones. The corn was placed between the stones. The top stone was turned on the bottom one until the grain was ground. Horses were used to turn some of the bigger millstones.

When more people came to the west, mills were built beside a stream. The mills had large water wheels. Running water from the stream outside the mill turned the water wheel. The water wheel was connected with the top millstone so that the millstone turned with the water wheel. People came from miles around to have their grain ground at the mill. The man who owned the mill was given part of the meal or flour as his pay.

The pioneers had a kind of a holiday coming to the mill. News and gossip from the different settlements were exchanged, and sometimes horses were swapped.

Corn meal was used to make many different kinds of bread and other dishes. Among them were:

Ash cake—Corn bread wrapped in cabbage leaves and baked in ashes.

Corn dodger—Corn meal and lard baked in lumps.

Hasty pudding—Corn meal mush; often eaten with milk or gravy or sweetened with maple sugar, honey, or molasses and used for a dessert.

Fried mush—Cold hasty pudding, sliced and fried in a skillet.

Hoe cake—Corn bread baked on the blade of a hoe. The hoe was taken off the handle, cleaned, and set in the coals.

Johnny cake—Usually made of corn meal, salt, boiling water, and milk. Some people added wheat flour if they had it; others added sugar or eggs. It was baked in an oven over the fireplace or in an iron pot with a cover or on a board in front of the fire.

Cook Some Corn Yourself

Roastin' Ears

Roasting must be done over an open fire. Ask your father or some other adult to help you. Select as many tender ears of fresh corn as needed. Pull back the husks from the ears but do not remove them. Clean all the silk from the ears of corn and then pull the husks back up to cover the ears completely. Soak the corn in cold water for thirty minutes. Place the ears on a bed of hot coals and cover with more hot coals. Roast them for thirty minutes. Remove the corn from the fire carefully, then remove husks and eat with salt and butter.

Hasty Pudding

3 cups of water
½ teaspoon of salt
½ cup of cornmeal

Put the water and salt in a saucepan. Bring it to a boil. Sprinkle the cornmeal into the boiling water a little at a time. Stir all the time so that it will not get lumpy. Cook for 45 minutes. Serve with milk and syrup.

Corn Pone

Measure one cup of sour milk and pour into a mixing bowl. Add enough corn meal and a little wheat flour until you have a thick batter. Add ½ teaspoon of salt and a tablespoon of melted shortening. Dissolve a teaspoon of soda in a small amount of water and add to the batter. Mix well. Pour into a greased pan and bake at 375° for about 25 minutes, or until golden brown.

Parched Corn

Put some dry field corn kernels in an iron skillet or in a covered iron kettle. Add some salt and butter. Parch over medium heat stirring constantly until golden brown.

Hominy

Put one quart of husked dry white field corn into two quarts of water. Add two tablespoonfuls of baking soda. Boil until the hulls of the grain come off easily. Wash in clear, cold water. Cook the hominy in milk seasoned to taste with butter and salt; or boil in water, and season to taste. It may be eaten with or without milk.

Vinegar

Apple cider and other fruit juices turn into vinegar when a slimy plant called mother of vinegar grows in them. Pioneers made their vinegar by letting cider, "worked preserves," old honey, and other sweets stand in a jar with a piece of mother of vinegar. They brought mother of vinegar with them from the East or got it from a neighbor. Vinegar was used for pickling cucumbers, beets, apples, onions, and some meats. It was used also in vinegar pie, a favorite dessert.

Make Vinegar Pie

Use prepared pie dough for the pie shell, or ask your mother to help you make one.

1 egg, well-beaten	4 tablespoons flour
3 tablespoons cider-vinegar	1 cup sugar
	1 cup boiling water
1 teaspoon lemon flavoring	1 baked pie shell

Mix sugar and flour thoroughly together, then add boiling water. Cook five minutes. Add well-beaten egg and cook in top of double boiler two minutes. Add lemon flavoring and vinegar. Pour into baked pie shell.

Sauerkraut

Part of the cabbage grown in the garden was often made into sauerkraut. The cabbage was cut into small pieces on a cabbage cutter—a board with sharp knife-like blades on it. The head of cabbage was rubbed back and fourth across the knives until it was all cut up. It was then mixed with salt and put in a big barrel or earthenware jar a layer at a time. Each layer was pressed down with a wooden pestle until brine or salty water came out of it. When all the cabbage was packed in, it was covered with a cloth and a board. A large stone was put on top of the board to keep the cabbage under the brine. The jar or barrel was set in a warm place so that bacteria would grow quickly in the mixture. This bateria made the cabbage ferment. After a few days the brine began to bubble. It did not have a very pleasant odor. The scum that came to the top was skimmed off. The cabbage was left to stand until it got sour. Then it was put in a cold place so the bacteria could not grow as fast. It was now ready to be used. When it was wanted for a meal, the necessary amount was taken out and cooked.

Butter

Cream was used to make butter. Whole milk was put in a shallow pan or dish. When the cream came to the top, it was skimmed off and saved until there was enough to be put in the churn for butter.

There were different kinds of churns. Some were little wooden barrels with handles that could be used to turn them around. Others were little barrels on rockers

that could be rocked back and forth. The kind of churn most often used, however, was a tall wooden or crockery jar with a cover that had a hole in the center. The hole was for the dasher. The dasher was a stick about the size of a broomstick with two little pieces of crossed wood fastened to the bottom. When the dasher was moved up and down through the hole in the cover, it splashed the cream. After a while butter would begin to form and float around in the churn. The butter came from the fat in the cream.

When all of the fat had come out of the cream, the dasher was taken out of the churn. The little lumps of butter were scooped out and put into a wooden bowl of very cold water. The butter was washed time and again with cold water and squeezed until all the milk was washed out. Then the butter was salted. It was kneaded with a paddle until the salt was well mixed with the butter.

The butter was next put into a butter mold. The mold was made of wood. It had a loose bottom with a handle. By moving the handle the butter could be pushed out of the mold. The bottom of most butter molds had a picture carved in it—an acorn, a strawberry, or some other familiar object. When the butter came out of the mold, it had a picture on the top. Those who had no butter mold made a smooth, round pat of butter on a plate.

Boys and girls liked to drink the buttermilk that was left in the churn when the butter was taken out.

Butter for You

If you wish to make butter, you must first make a small churn. Use a quart jar with a cover. Make a hole in the center of the cover. Make a dasher of smooth round stick that will go through the hole. Fasten two small flat pieces of wood to the bottom of the stick.

Put two cups of heavy cream in the jar and then put the cover on. Work the dasher up and down until little lumps of butter appear. When no more butter seems to be forming, take off the cover and scoop out the bits of butter. Place the butter in a dish of cold water and wash out all the milk. Salt the butter and shape it into a smooth pat.

Cottage Cheese

Some pioneers used their extra milk to make cottage cheese. The milk was allowed to stand in a warm place until it soured and curds formed. Then it was put into a cloth bag and hung up until the liquid or *whey* had all drained out. The curd that was left was put into a dish and salted. This was cottage cheese.

Sometimes the cottage cheese was made into round balls about as big as a child's fist. These were put in a warm place to cure or ripen; that is, to turn yellow and become more firm and sharper tasting. When the cheese had ripened all the way through, it was ready to eat. This was called hand cheese.

Cooked cheese was made by putting cottage cheese into a bowl and letting it stand until it was yellow and smelly. Then it was cooked with eggs and caraway seed and spread on bread to be eaten.

Make Cottage Cheese

Cottage cheese is easy to make. You can do it like this: Let one quart of milk stand in a warm place until it becomes thick and sour. Pour the sour milk into a pan, place on the stove, and heat very slowly until the whey or watery part comes to the top. Pour off the whey. Put the white curd that is left into a cloth bag. Hang it up, and let it drip for about six hours. Then take it out of the bag and put it into a bowl. Add one-half a teaspoon of salt and mix well. The cheese is now ready to serve.

Apples

At first the pioneers had very few apples, but as soon as they settled in a new place they planted apple trees. When the trees grew large enough, there was plenty of the fruit.

There were several ways of using the apples. Pioneer women made apple butter by cooking apples with sugar or honey in a big kettle out of doors. A long wooden paddle with holes in it was used to stir the apple mixture. It was cooked until very thick.

Some pioneers made apple leather. The apples were peeled, sliced, and cooked to a very thick mush. This was spread out in a thin layer on a board or cloth to dry. In winter the dry apple leather was cooked with water.

Many pioneers dried apples. They peeled the apples and cut out the cores. Then they sliced the apples cross-wise into rings. The rings were put on a string and hung up to dry. Drying took several days. The apples were covered with some kind of netting to keep off insects. When they were dry they were left hanging or were stored away until they were needed. Children liked to eat pieces of dried apple, but most dried apples were cooked with water and used in pies.

Some hard apples were put into a hole in the ground and covered with straw and dirt to keep them from freezing. In winter the fresh apples could be dug out and used as needed.

When apples were scarce and hard to get, the pioneers found that the pumpkin could be used instead in many of the same ways. Pumpkins were used in pies and to make a spread for bread. They were dried or made into pumpkin butter or pumpkin leather to keep them from spoiling.

Preserve Some Apples or Pumpkin

Dried apples may be prepared quite easily. Choose as many nice firm apples as you wish to dry. Take out the cores and slice the apples crosswise into rings about half an inch thick. Put the rings on strings and hang them in a sunny place until the apples are very dry. This may take several days. The apples should be brought inside each night. They should be covered with a piece

of netting as they dry. This will keep off insects. Or, you can slice the apples and spread them on a board to dry instead of cutting them into rings.

Dried pumpkin rings are made in almost the same way. Wash the pumpkin very carefully. Cut it in half crosswise. Take out all the seeds. Cut each half into rings about three-fourths of an inch thick. Put the rings around a pole—an old broomstick is good for this. Find something to support the ends of the pole. You might lay it across the backs of two straight chairs, or you could use two forked sticks. Put the pumpkin in the sun until it is very dry.

To cook your dried apple or pumpkin, soak the pieces in water until they are soft. Cook them until tender in just enough water to cover them. Add as much sugar as you like.

Apple leather is made like this. Wash as many apples as you wish to make into leather. Peel the apples. Cut them into eighths and take out the seeds and cores. Put the apples into a saucepan. Add water so that it half covers the apples. Cook the apples until they are a *very* thick mush. Spread the cooked apples on a clean cloth and let dry. The drying will take two or three days.

Pumpkin butter is also easy to make. Wash a pumpkin. Cut it into pieces and peel each piece. Put the pieces into a saucepan. Add enough water to about half cover the pumpkin. Let it cook until it is soft and mushy. Then press it through a colander (sieve) to take out all the lumps. Measure the cooked pumpkin to see how many cups you have. Add one cup of sugar or honey for every two cups of pumpkin. Also add one-fourth of a teaspoon of cinnamon or ginger per cup. Cook the mixture until it is very thick.

THRESHING TIME

As more land was cleared, many pioneer farmers planted wheat. When the grain was ripe, it was harvested and then it had to be threshed or separated from the stalks. Threshing time was late in the summer.

Threshing was done with a tool called a flail. It was made from two sticks, one about three feet long and the other four feet. The sticks were tied together at one end with strips of leather.

When the wheat was harvested, it was tied with bands into bundles called sheaves. At threshing time a couple of sheaves of grain at a time were laid on the threshing floor with the heads together. The bands were cut. Then the flail was swung so that the sticks came down right on the heads of the sheaves. The grain was beaten, turned over, and beaten again until all the grain was free from the straw.

The straw was lifted and shaken with a pitchfork and then thrown to the side. The kernels of grain and the chaff were piled in a heap with a scoop shovel. Four sheaves usually made one peck of grain. Four pecks made a bushel. One man could thresh about ten bushels in one day.

78

After threshing, the grain had to be screened to separate the kernels from the chaff. This was done with *riddles*, objects that looked something like coarse sieves. The riddles were made of sheepskin thongs woven criss-cross on wooden hoops. Four different kinds of riddles were used to screen the grain. The first one had big openings, the next a little smaller, and the third was just big enough to let the grain go through.

When the grain was put in the fourth riddle it could not go through at all; any remaining dust sifted through the holes and the clean kernels of grain were left in the riddle. The clean grain was stored in barrels until needed.

THE PIONEER SCHOOL

When the pioneer farm had been developed to the point where the family lived fairly comfortably, and when several families had settled in the same area, it was time to start a school.

The school building was built of logs in much the same way that cabins were built. It usually had only one room, and pupils in all grades studied together. Boys sat on one side of the room, and girls on the other. The seats were benches without backs. These were made by splitting logs about eight to ten inches in diameter in half. The halves were smoothed with a draw knife, and then holes were bored in the curved sides and wooden pins inserted for legs. By varying the size of the pins, benches of various heights could be made for children of different ages. In the wall just under the windows, holes were bored at a slight downward angle. Wooden pins inserted into these holes supported wide boards, smoothed so that they could be used for writing. Pupils took turns working at the writing desks.

The children often had to walk long distances to get to the school. It was generally open only two or three months during the year, at the time when there was not much work to be done on the farm.

The teacher was seldom well trained. If he could read, spell, write well enough to "set copies," and do all the sums in arithmetic he was considered qualified to teach. His pay was very low. He usually "boarded, round"; that is, spend a few days in the home of each of his pupils.

Learning the ABC's was the first task of the student. When he knew the letters of the alphabet by sight, he was taught to spell simple words. When the child could spell fairly well, he began the First Reader. When he had reached the Second Reader, he was ready to learn to write. He wrote with a quill pen in a copy-book. The teacher wrote a line at the top of the page, and the child copied it below. This line was often one that was intended to teach a moral lesson as well as provide an example of penmanship. Arithmetic, often called "ciphering," came with the Third Reader.

The teacher sat in front of the room and called each group of children in turn to stand before him and recite.

They often said their lessons aloud together. Children who did not know their lessons or who did not behave were made to sit in a corner wearing a dunce cap.

Test Yourself

Almost 100 years ago these arithmetic problems appeared in arithmetic textbooks for the pupils to work without the help of a teacher. Can you work them? (The answers are given at the bottom of page eighty-five). ——————————

1. If 12 horses eat up 30 bushels of oats in a week, how many bushels will serve 45 horses the same time? ——————————

2. Two farmers bartered: A had 120 bushels of wheat, at $1.50 per bushel, for which B gave him 100 bushels of barley, worth .65 per bushel, and the balance in oats at .40 per bushel. What quantity of oats did A receive from B? _____

3. Three partners, A, B, and C shipped 108 mules from the West-Indies; of which A owned 48; B, 36; and C, 24. But in stress of weather, the mariners were obliged to throw 45 of them overboard. I demand how much of the loss each owner must sustain? _____

4. The metric system was legalized in France in 1795; its use was enforced by law in 1845. If half as much time shall elapse between the time it was legalized in this country (1866) and the time it shall be enforced, in what

year will its use be enforced here?

---

5. At 60 cents per hundred, what will be the cost of ice for a family that takes 40 pounds 3 times a week, from April 1 to October 7? _____

6. Can you divide 25 apples between two persons, so as to give one 7 more than the other? _____

7. Jane checked the change in her purse and said, "This is strange. I have 60 cents all in nickels and dimes and there are twice as many nickels as dimes." How many nickels and dimes did Jane have? _____

8. If it costs 75 cents a cord to saw wood, so as to make each stick into 3 parts, what will it cost to saw it so as to make each stick into 4 parts?

THE PIONEER CHURCH

The first settlers in the West were very busy making homes in the wilderness. The families were scattered and neighbors might be several miles apart. There were no churches for many years. The first ministers to come to the new land were called circuit riders. They traveled about on horseback, visiting the pioneer cabins and holding services. Each covered a certain territory and followed a regular route in his travels over his territory or circuit. It took several weeks or even months to visit everyone on the circuit. The people were usually glad to see the circuit rider. Sometimes he was the only visitor a family would have for two weeks at a time. The circuit rider might also sell Bibles and other books. The Bible was usually the first and sometimes the only book to be found in a pioneer cabin.

During the summer many of the circuit riders held camp meetings. These were religious services held out of doors. Whole families, bringing with them their

tents and their food, came to the meeting place and camped while services were being held. Camp meetings often began on Friday afternoon and lasted until noon on Monday, but they might be longer or shorter. These meetings were very popular. The people enjoyed getting away from their work for a few days to attend the services and to see their neighbors and make new friends. Some families would travel as much as fifty miles to attend a camp meeting.

As more people moved into a community and the land became fairly well settled, church buildings were built. These churches were small. One minister usually served several churches and held services for each at different times. Each church might have services only once or twice a month.

The worshippers sang without books or music to guide them. Evening services began at "candlelighting." There were no lamps but each family brought a tallow candle. As they entered the church, the families lighted their candles and placed them in holders along the wall.

PLAYTIME FOR THE PIONEER

Although the early settlers had to work very hard, they were able to find some time for fun. Often when neighbors gathered together to help each other with some of the work, they made a party of it. There were quilting bees, husking bees, corn shellings, house raisings, stump pullings, harvestings, and threshings. As they worked, the people visited with each other and caught up on the news. When they had finished the work, there was always plenty of food.

Holidays and special days were also times for recreation for the pioneer. Christmas was a very important day for them. The gifts exchanged by the members of the family were few in number and of a practical sort, usually such things as mittens, stockings, mufflers, caps, and the like. Sometimes a little girl found some beads in the toe of her stocking, and a boy might find a brand new jack-knife. But there was always plenty of food. Many days were spent in preparing for the holiday. A dozen or more pies might be made and put out to freeze; batches of cookies made beforehand; apples and nuts put on the table.

Singing was a favorite activity. You may know some of the old songs such as "Wait for the Wagon," "The Quilting Party," "Paper of Pins," or "Go Tell Aunt Nancy." The words of some songs didn't always make a lot of sense, but the pioneer liked to sing them.

Dancing was very popular, too. It was the kind of dancing we know as square dancing and folk dancing. Pioneer boys and girls knew such dance terms as *balance and swing, allemanda left, grand right and left, all promenade, circle four, birdie in the cage, dive for the oyster, duck for the clam, splitting the ring,* and many more from the time they were very young.

Some dances were held out of doors. The ground was smoothed and rolled until it was firm; then swept clean for the dancing surface. Other times dances were held in the cabins. When this was the case, the bedstead, loom, table, spinning wheel, and other furniture was moved outside—and wooden logs were arranged along the cabin walls for seats. Dances might also be held in barns.

Sing Some Pioneer Songs

PAPER OF PINS

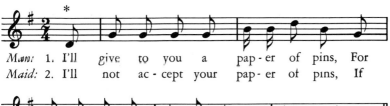

Man: 1. I'll give to you a pap-er of pins, For
Maid: 2. I'll not ac-cept your pap-er of pins, If

that's the way true love be-gins, If you will mar-ry
that's the way true love be-gins, For I'll not mar-ry

me, miss, If you will mar - ry me.
you, sir, For I'll not mar - ry you.

*Rhythm should be adjusted for each stanza.

2.

I'll give to you a little brown
   dog
To lie in your lap when you
   ride abroad,
If you will marry me, miss,
If you will marry me.

I'll not accept your little
   brown dog
To lie in my lap when I ride
   abroad,

For I'll not marry you, sir,
For I'll not marry you.

3.

I'll give to you a dress of red
All stitched around with
   golden thread,
If you will marry me, miss,
If you will marry me.

I'll not accept your dress of
   red
All stitched around with

91

golden thread,
For I'll not marry you, sir,
For I'll not marry you.

4.
I'll give to you a coach and
 six
With every horse as black as
 pitch,
If you will marry me, miss,
If you will marry me.

I'll not accept your coach
 and six
With every horse as black as
 pitch,
For I'll not marry you, sir,
For I'll not marry you.

5.
I'll give to you the key to
 my chest
That you may have gold at
 your request,

If you will marry me, miss,
If you will marry me.

I'll not accept the key to
 your chest
That I may have gold at my
 request,
For I'll not marry you, sir,
For I'll not marry you.

6.
I'll give to you my hand and
 heart
That we may love and never
 part,
If you will marry me, miss,
If you will marry me.

I will accept your hand and
 heart
That we may love and never
 part,
And I will marry you, sir,
And I will marry you.

GO TELL AUNT NANCY

1. Go tell Aunt Nan - cy, Go tell Aunt Nan - cy,

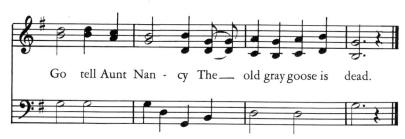

Go tell Aunt Nan - cy The— old gray goose is dead.

2.

The one she'd been saving,
The one she'd been saving,
The one she'd been saving,
To make a feather bed.

3.

She died last Friday,
She died last Friday,
She died last Friday,
With a pain all in her head.

4.

Old gander's weeping,
Old gander's weeping,
Old gander's weeping,
Because his wife is dead.

5.

The goslings are mourning,
The goslings are mourning,
The goslings are mourning,
Because their mother's dead.

QUILTING PARTY

In the sky the bright stars glit-tered,— On the bank the pale moon shone; And 'twas from Aunt Di - na's quilt - ing par - ty I was see - ing Nel - lie

home. _____ I was see - ing Nel - lie

home. _____ I was see - ing Nel - lie home.

WAIT FOR THE WAGON

It's Ev - 'ry Sun - day morn - ing, When I am by your side;

We'll jump in - to the wag - on and all_ take a ride.

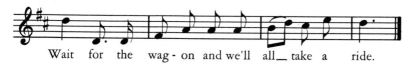

Wait for the wag - on, Wait for the wag - on,

Wait for the wag - on and we'll all_ take a ride.

Going to Jerusalem

Arrange the chairs in two rows with the backs together, one chair less than the number of players. All players but one are seated in chairs. He is the leader. The leader marches around the chairs saying, "Going to Jerusalem! Going to Jerusalem!" When he wishes, he stops in front of a player and taps three times on the floor. This is a signal for the player to follow him. The leader continues to stop in front of players until all are marching. Then the music starts. The players march around the rows of chairs until the music stops or some other signal is given. Then they all hurry for a chair. The player without a chair is out of the game. He takes a chair from the group as he leaves. The game continues until only a few are left marching. The players out of the game may clap for the marching.

The game may be played without a leader, the players all ready to march in the first part of the game. In a schoolroom with seats, the players may march up one aisle and down the next aisle, and so on. The seat that is not used may be marked by placing something on the desk.

Puss in a Corner

Station children around the room by table, chairs, doors, desk, or anything serving as corners. Puss goes from one child to another saying, "Pussy wants a corner." The child approached replies, "Go to my next-door neighbor." The other children beckon to each other and try to exchange corners when Puss is not looking. If Puss can get a corner, then the child left out becomes Puss.

Three Deep

The players form a double circle, the players in both circles facing the center of the circle. Two players acting as runner and chaser are stationed on the outside of the circle. At a signal, the chaser starts after the runner. The runner may escape being tagged by stepping in front of any couple. When he does this, the person on the back of the file of three becomes the runner and may be tagged by the chaser. When the chaser tags the runner, the runner becomes chaser and tries to tag him. Running through the circle is permissible, but the runner may not stop within the circle except to stop in front of another couple to escape being tagged.

Play Some Musical Games

SHOO FLY

Shoo fly, don't both-er me, Shoo fly, don't both-er me,

Shoo fly, don't both - er me, For I be-long to

some-bod - y, I do, I do, I do, And I

ain't got - ta tell you who, For I be-long to

some -bod - y, Yes, in - deed, I do.

Directions for Shoo Fly

Group breaks up into couples and forms a single circle of couples.

1. All join hands and take four steps toward the center.
2. Take four steps back to original position.
3. Four steps in.
4. Four steps back.
5—8 (Songs may be repeated if necessary). Keep

hands joined. One couple lifts inside hands to form an arch. One couple on the opposite side of the circle starts across leading every one else, hands joined under the arch, until finally the couple making the arch turn under their own hands, keeping the circle intact with all players facing out.

Repeat 1-4 taking four steps backward toward the center of the circle and four steps forward to places.

Repeat 5-8 to turn circle right side out again. All players walk backward during this part.

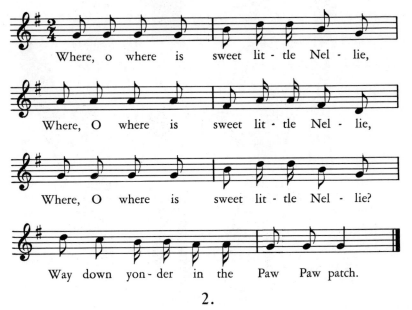

Where, o where is sweet lit - tle Nel - lie,

Where, O where is sweet lit - tle Nel - lie,

Where, O where is sweet lit - tle Nel - lie?

Way down yon - der in the Paw Paw patch.

2.

Come on, boys, let's go find her,
Come on, boys, let's go find her,
Come on, boys, let's go find her,
Way down yonder in the pawpaw patch.

3.

Pickin' up pawpaws, puttin' 'em in her pocket,
Pickin' up pawpaws, puttin' 'em in her pocket,
Pickin' up pawpaws, puttin' 'em in her pocket,
Way down yonder in the pawpaw patch.

100

The formation for this game is the same as for the Virginia Reel, two lines of players face each other. The first verse is sung using the name of the person at the head of one line. During the singing this person turns to the right and skips down behind his own line and on around the other and back to his place. As the second verse is sung, the same person skips around in line again followed by all the people in the other line until all are back in place again. All sing the third verse as the first ones in each line join hands, the second ones join hands, etc., and all follow the head couple around the set and back to place again. Then the head couple moves down the outside of the set to the foot, the next couple becomes the head. Repeat for each turn. If a boy is at the head of the line, the group may sing, "Where, oh, where is poor little Willie," etc.

SKIP TO MY LOU

Form a single circle of partners, facing in. An extra player (two or three in a large circle) is without a partner inside the circle. All sing and clap in time to a verse started by the player in the center. This player steals someone's partner and skips with her (hands joined in skating position) all around the circle and back to her place. The player left without a partner quickly chooses another, and the games continue in this manner.

1. I've lost my gal, now what - 'll I do;
Cho. Skip, skip, skip to my Lou;

I've lost my gal, now what - 'll I do;
Skip, skip, skip to my Lou;

I've lost my gal, now what - 'll I do?
Skip, skip, skip to my Lou;

Skip to my Lou, my dar - ling.
Skip to my Lou, my dar - ling.

*Rhythm should be adjusted for each stanza.

2.

I'll get another one, purtier too;
I'll get another one, purtier too,
I'll get another one, purtier too,
Skip to my Lou, my darling.

3.

That boy wears a number ten shoe . . .

4.

He's got big feet and awkward too . . .

5.

I'm right upset, say what'll I do . . .

6.

Flies in the sugarbowl, shoo fly, shoo . . .

7.

Bears in the pantry, boo, boo, boo . . .

8.

Mules in the cellar, kicking up through . . .

9.

Pups in the buttermilk, what'll I do . . .

10.

Cows in the cornfield, two by two . . .

11.

Skunks in the parlor, phew, phew, phew . . .

12.

Cat in the cream crock, skim him through . . .

13.

Owls in the tree top, hoo, hoo, hoo . . .

14.

We'll keep it up 'til half past two . . .

15.

I'll get her back in spite of you . . .

16.

Purty as a red bird, purtier too . . .

17.

When I go courting, I take two . . .

18.

Pig in a poke, say who is who . . .

19.
Sugar is sweet and so are you . . .
20.
My gal wears a number nine shoe . . .
21.
Little red wagon, painted blue . . .
22.
Hurry up, slow poke, do oh do . . .
23.
Gone again, now what'll I do . . .
24.
Can't get a fat gal, skinny one'll do . . .
25.
One eye brown, and one eye blue . . .
26.
She's the one I want to woo . . .
27.
She's my gal I love her true . . .
28.
She'll have a dress of brightest blue . . .
29.
Get a white horse and a cutter too . . .
30.
We will marry 'fore its through.

THE PIONEER SPIRIT

The life of the pioneer was not easy but he felt that it was a good life. Through hard work he was able to develop his land so that it provided food and clothing for his family. He was able to make for himself the kind of life that he wanted. Instead of complaining about the things he did not have, he found ways of using the materials around him to supply his needs.

Many of the skills of the pioneer folk are all but forgotten today. In a few places far away from the cities people still follow some of the old ways, but most people take advantage of more convenient, modern methods for providing food, clothing, and shelter. There are few parts of our country where people need to live as pioneers.

Although we do not live as the pioneers did, the pioneer spirit is still alive today. Now as always there are people who are working to build a new and better life. They are the pioneers in science, education, the arts; those who are not afraid to try new things. It was this spirit which helped to build our country and which continues to build down through the years.

INDEX